the very short, entirely true

HISTORY of MERMAIDS

by SARAH LASKOW

illustrated by REIMENA YEE

Penguin Workshop

[redacted]

HAVE YOU ever looked out at the tumbling waves of the bright blue ocean and thought about living underwater? Have you dreamed about swimming free through the ocean's depths?

Have you ever imagined meeting a mermaid?

Most likely, the mermaid you imagine is beautiful, with long hair and a charming voice. But a mermaid might also have small, mean eyes and sharp teeth. Would she help people if they were drowning? Or would she try to sink their ships?

Throughout time, people have had many different ideas about mermaids.

No one has ever found proof that mermaids exist. But for thousands of years, people have been telling stories about the half-human, half-fish residents of the oceans.

This is the true history of mermaids—the story of all the reasons people thought they were real and how they became part of our world.

WHAT DOES *the* "MER" *in* *MERMAID* MEAN?

AROUND THE world, there are many names for mermaids. Look, for instance, at the British Isles, which include Great Britain, Ireland, and all the small islands around them. In Ireland, mermaids are known as *merrows* or *murúcha*. On the Isle of Man, they're *ben-varrey*, and in the Orkney Islands, *finfolk*. Old English has its own word for a mermaid—she's a *merewif*. And that's just in one small corner of the globe.

Islands are natural places for tales of mermaids to grow—they're surrounded by water! But sailors brought back stories of fish-people from their faraway travels, so countries that sent ships out to sea have mermaid myths, too.

Why do we call these creatures *mermaids* today? Like mermaids themselves, the word has two parts. One half is easy to understand: The word *maid* used to mean "young woman." But what about *mer*?

Mer comes from a word in Old English, *mere*, which means "lake" or "sea." Words often change their shape over time, as people say them over and over again. But they still mean the same thing. The Old English *mere* came from an even older word for the sea, *meer*.

Join *meer* and *maid*, and you have a young woman of the sea. A mermaid!

ORKNEY
ISLANDS
NORTH
SEA
SCOTLAND
NORTHERN
IRELAND
ISLE OF MAN
IRELAND
IRISH
SEA
ENGLAND
WALES
ENGLISH
CHANNEL

ANCIENT LEGENDS, MANY MERMAIDS

STORIES OF fish-people go back thousands of years. In those earliest stories, mermaids and mermen were gods.

OANNES

Ancient Babylonians had legends about a group of godlike beings who were part fish and part human. At first, they appeared as fish, with human voices. But underneath their fish heads, they also had human heads. They had human feet hiding near their tails, too.

One of these fish-men was named Oannes, and he was friendly to humans—he taught them about writing and science. One of the first images ever made of a merperson was a picture of Oannes, carved on the walls of a palace.

DERCETO

Syrians had a sadder myth about a goddess who became a mermaid. She was named Derceto, and she fell in love with a mortal. Soon, they had a baby. Derceto was embarrassed and upset that she had given birth to a human child. To escape, she tried to drown herself in a lake. But she didn't die. Instead, she became part woman, part fish.

MATSYA

In India's Hindu mythology, there is a story about a small fish named Matsya who asks Manu, one of the earliest men, to protect him. In exchange, Matsya promises, he will save Manu from a dangerous flood. Manu agrees. He keeps the little creature safe in a jar, until it grows into a giant fish.

One day, Matsya announces that the flood is coming and reveals that he's actually a god—Vishnu, who keeps the world peaceful and in order. He tells Manu to build a boat. When the storm begins, he attaches it to the fish, which carries Manu to safety, high on a mountain.

In art, Matsya appears as a merman who has a fish tail and a human upper body—but four arms!

TRITON

In Greek mythology, Triton, son of the sea god Poseidon, had a fish's tail. He was the color of the sea and wore seashells on his shoulders. He lived in a golden castle under the water, and he had a conch shell that he blew to control the waves or to announce his father's arrival.

NOMMOS

The Dogon people, who live in West Africa, have a myth about the Nommos, part-fish gods born at the beginning of the world. They came from the sky, gave humans knowledge, and then returned to their home near the star Sirius.

MERMAID, MERMAN, *on the* WALL

MORE THAN 2,700 years ago, one of the first pictures of a merperson was carved to illustrate these ancient myths.

In 721 BC, Sargon II became king of Assyria, a region covering what is now Iraq, Iran, and part of Turkey. As king, Sargon had a palace built in the city of Dur-Sharrukin. The walls were made from slabs of stone, with pictures of battles, performances, and myths carved into them.

Among the figures was the wise fish-man from ancient legend, sometimes called Oannes. He was an important god who gave humanity the knowledge to survive and form a civilization.

the POWER *of* MAMI WATA

MERMAID GODS and goddesses aren't only ancient history, though. Plenty of people around the world today believe in Mami Wata, a water goddess whose story began in Africa.

To her followers, Mami Wata is a powerful goddess who will bring them love, strength, and wealth. They believe in her, hoping to become rich—or simply to get everything they need.

Like all gods, Mami Wata works in ways that are sometimes mysterious. For example, Mami Wata might kidnap one of her followers and take them to her ocean world. It can be a frightening experience. But they return, blessed with wisdom and understanding.

Mami Wata has other names, too. Some people call her La Sirene, and others call her Yemanja.

And she can take many forms. Sometimes she is a woman with a snake around her neck. Snakes are often linked to African water spirits, and Mami Wata is known as a snake charmer. Sometimes, Mami Wata is a hybrid fish-goat-woman.

But often she's shown as a mermaid, with a woman's body and a fish's tail.

a SIREN'S DANGEROUS SONG

OF ALL the stories about mermaids, one of the most famous comes from ancient Greece. The Greeks had their myth about fish-tailed Triton, but they also told of sirens, creatures who lived on a rocky island in the sea. When a boat passed by, the sirens would make beautiful music. The sound was so powerful that sailors would start heading toward it.

But this was a mistake. The sirens were said to be surrounded by piles of human bones. They would destroy the men they captured, although no one knew exactly how. Perhaps the men forgot about everything but the sirens' songs and stopped eating. Maybe the sirens killed them. The only thing that was clear was that these creatures were deadly.

A Greek man named Odysseus (say: O-DI-see-us) knew how dangerous the sirens were. He told his crew to block their ears when their ship passed the sirens' island.

But Odysseus wanted to hear the sirens sing. He had his men tie him to the ship's mast. The music he heard was so irresistible that he tried to jump overboard and swim to the sirens' island. The ropes held him tight, though, and he made it safely past the island. He survived hearing the sirens' song.

Ancient Greeks imagined the sirens as ugly monsters—part woman, part bird. Over time, the idea of what the sirens might look like changed. Sometimes artists would show them as half-fish or give them both fish tails and bird claws.

Today, when the story of the sirens is told, they're often pictured as mermaids. But that doesn't make them less deadly to sailors who hear their enchanting song.

MERMEN *vs.* MERMAIDS

THE GREEK story of the sirens helped mermaids become famous around the world. But to some people, mermen were equally frightening.

Mermen were often thought to be more dangerous than mermaids. Stories that originated in the British Isles described them as having green skin, narrow eyes, and gloomy faces.

Mermen were usually wary of humans. In many stories, they'd send their mermaid wives onto land to earn silver, while they stayed behind in the sea.

Though they preferred the water, mermen did like to interfere in the human world. They were sometimes said to sneak near boats and steal fishermen's bait and fish. Some fishermen believed that mermen would grab their fishing lines, too.

But they could also treat humans fairly. In one folktale from Norway, a fisherman is out at sea when he sees a shivering merman in the water. He gives the merman one of his mittens to help keep him warm. The merman disappears without a word.

Later he reappears to warn the fisherman about an approaching storm. The sea looks calm, but the fisherman decides to believe the merman. He rows back home. Sure enough, a dangerous storm blows in, and the fisherman realizes that the merman saved his life.

MISCHIEVOUS MERMAIDS *in* ASIA *and* AUSTRALIA

SOME MYTHICAL creatures are found in just one part of the world. But people all around the globe tell stories about mermaids. Mermaids in Asia and Australia aren't so different from mermaids in Europe and Africa.

SUVANNAMACCHA

Thailand has a popular story about a mermaid princess named Suvannamaccha. Her name means "golden fish," and her father is a demon who, in one famous story, captured the goddess Sita.

Hanuman, a monkey god, is given the job of rescuing Sita. He starts trying to build a bridge to reach her island prison. But the bridge keeps disappearing!

At first, Hanuman doesn't understand what's happening. But he soon discovers that mermaids, led by Suvannamaccha, keep stealing the rocks he's using to build the bridge. Only Suvannamaccha can tell them to stop.

Hanuman tries to catch her, but she keeps swimming away. And so he comes up with a new plan. He starts telling Suvannamaccha how beautiful and charming she is. And Suvannamaccha allows him to get closer. She decides he's strong and handsome, and she begins to fall in love. Against her father's orders, she agrees to help him rescue Sita.

NINGYO

Not all mermaids are beautiful. In Japan, the *ningyo* had the body of a fish and the head of a man or monkey, with sharp little teeth. It was thought that if a person was lucky enough to eat *ningyo* meat, they would live for many years. One young girl, according to legend, was given only one bite and lived to be eight hundred!

But beware: When you catch a *ningyo*, dangerous storms could be approaching.

YAWKYAWKS

In Australia, there are mermaids called *yawkyawks*—"young women spirit beings"—who are said to live in freshwater ponds. Their hair is green and looks like seaweed. Some are part fish; others are part crocodile or even part snake. Whatever creature they resemble, at night their tails can transform into legs! They leave their ponds and explore the dry land.

Yawkyawks are usually gentle with humans. They protect our drinking water, and they can make it rain. Most times, rain is a welcome resource. But like *ningyo*, *yawkyawks* are connected to terrible storms. Make a *yawkyawk* angry, and she might bring not just rain, but a flood.

the MYSTERIOUS MERMAID BONES *of* JAPAN

ALL THE way back in the year 1222, a strange body washed up on Kyushu, in the south of Japan. Could it have been a *ningyo*? The people of the city believed the bones were a sign of good luck, and they buried them at a temple.

Hundreds of years later, around the 1770s, the bones were dug up. For decades after, people in the temple would soak the bones in water and distribute the water to summer visitors. It was supposed to have the power to keep people from getting sick.

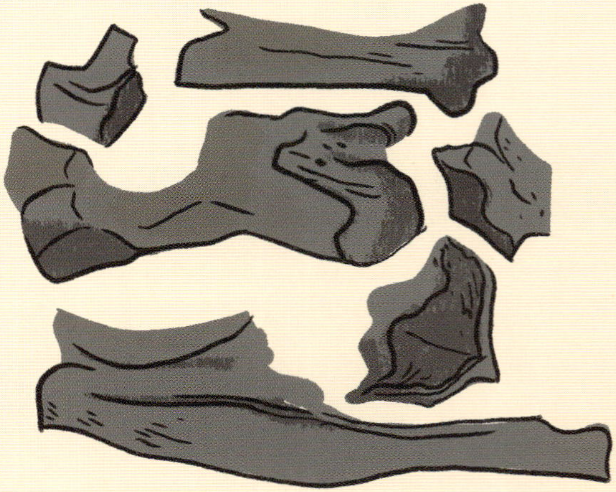

Today, the temple still has six of those bones. They're worn down and smooth, because so many people have touched them over the centuries.

There's another place in Japan to see the remains of a *ningyo*, too. It's in the Tenshou-Kyousha shrine, a religious building not far from Mount Fuji, Japan's tallest mountain. Inside a wood and glass case, there is a small dried merman mummy on display. It looks like a little old man, hunched over and standing on a curved fish tail.

According to legend, a fisherman trespassed in protected waters, and as punishment, he was turned into a *ningyo*. Like any merman, he had the head of a man and the body of a fish. In the story, at the end of his life, the *ningyo* met a prince and told him the sad tale. He asked the prince to keep his body and preserve it as a warning so that no one else would make the same mistake of fishing where they shouldn't.

MERMAID SIGHTINGS

CHRISTOPHER COLUMBUS
1451–1506

EVEN THOUGH mermaids and mermen have a long history in myth and legend, people who lived near the sea or who sailed on the ocean were convinced mermaids weren't just stories. They often reported seeing mermaids in the water. To sailors, mermaids were as real as any other incredible sea creature.

This has been going on for hundreds of years. Christopher Columbus claimed his crew spotted mermaids—but he was *not* impressed! After sailing across the Atlantic Ocean, Columbus's ships arrived at a group of islands in the Caribbean. One day, an admiral reported that three creatures had risen up out of the water—definitely mermaids, he said. In 1493 Columbus wrote that mermaids are "not as pretty" as they had expected, "for somehow in the face they look like men."

About one hundred years after Columbus, British explorer Henry Hudson reported seeing a mermaid in the Atlantic Ocean. She had "very white" skin, long black hair hanging down her back, and a tail like a dolphin's, he wrote.

Mermaids were spotted by sailors all over the world, in rivers, along the coasts, and in the middle of the seas.

a MAP *of* MERMAIDS

Wherever sailors traveled, they returned with stories of mermaids they had spotted all over the world. Often, these reports came from the coasts of faraway islands, but it was also common for sailors to say they had seen mermaids in the seas around Great Britain and Scandinavia. This went on for centuries! One of the earliest written accounts of a mermaid sighting comes from two thousand years ago, when the area in and around France was called Gaul. But as recently as the 1880s, a mermaid was reportedly seen in a river in Pennsylvania. Even today, people sometimes think they see mermaids sunning themselves on beaches or sitting on rocky coastlines.

Faroe Islands
1670
Norway
1608
Scotland
1747
Denmark
1749
Ireland
558, 887
Holland
1403
Isle of Man
1800
Gaul
100s
Europe
Asia
Africa
Ceylon
1560
Borneo
1718
Cape of Good Hope
1641

LIFE *on* LAND

IN FOLKTALES, men often caught mermaids by tricking them. These stories always begin with the mermaid hiding a special object on land in order to take a human form and sneak into human places. Sometimes it's a magical hood or tight-fitting cap made of red feathers that she removes from her head. Sometimes she leaves behind her fish skin. Without her hood or fish skin, a mermaid would never be able to return to the ocean.

But in these stories, the man who finds the object steals it. The thief demands the mermaid stay on dry land and become his wife. But this plot never works out. The mermaid finds her one special object and returns to the sea, often taking her children (and sometimes her husband) with her.

One mermaid had a better experience with life on land. According to the local history of Edam, a town in the Netherlands, a mermaid actually lived there in the early fifteenth century. She lost her way in a storm and was found by two women. They gave her a dress and taught her how to spin yarn and to weave. But they could not teach her to speak.

Not all mermaids do so well out of water, though. In the eighteenth century, Dutch writers reported that a mermaid was caught on the island of Amboine (or Amboina) in what is now Indonesia. According to their accounts, the mermaid was five feet long, had pink hairs running along its green tail, and refused to eat—not fish, not crab, not lobsters. It died in a tub four days and seven hours after it was caught.

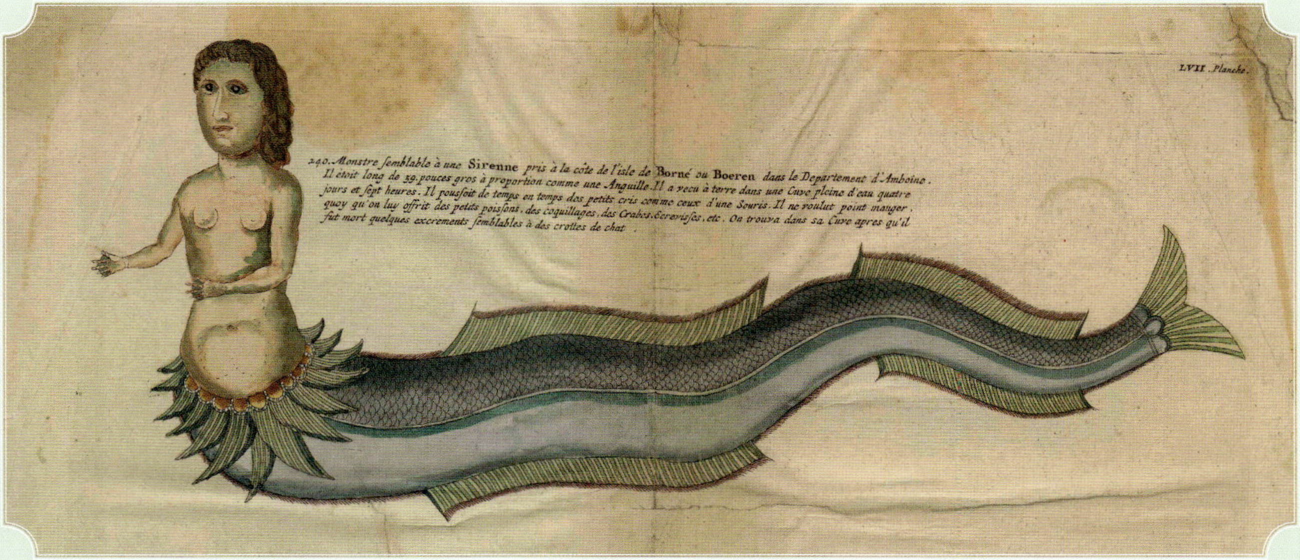

REAL-LIFE MERMAIDS

SOME MERMAID experts believe that the mermaid caught in Amboine in the 1700s was actually a dugong, an unusual type of mammal that lives underwater. A similar creature, the manatee, may have inspired at least some of the mermaid sightings that sailors reported, as well.

MANATEES

Big gray manatees live in coastal waters along the United States' eastern edge, in Central and South America, around Caribbean islands, and on Africa's western coast. They spend much of their time scooting along the seafloor and, just by eating grass, can grow to about ten feet long and one thousand pounds.

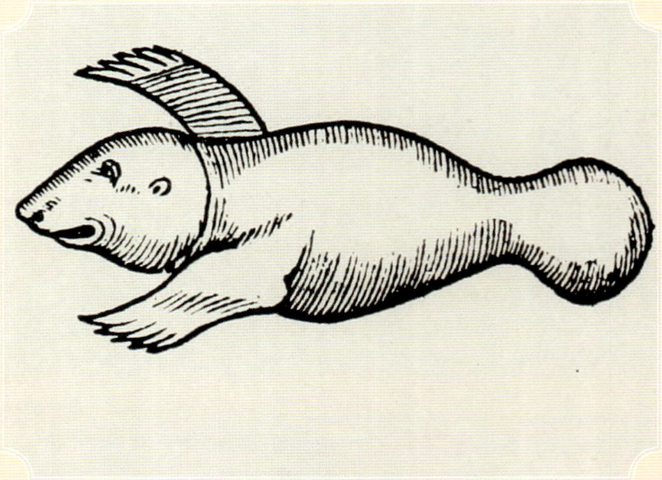

Manatees belong to an order of animals called Sirenia, named after the mythical sirens. But they're much less dangerous and have few natural enemies. When a manatee meets an alligator, for instance, it might gently bump the alligator as a way of asking it to move. And the alligator will!

Sometimes manatees stand on their tails and lift their chests out of the water. They don't look much like humans, but maybe, from very far away, sailors saw them and thought they were half-people, half-fish.

DUGONGS

Dugongs are similar to manatees, but they have a longer life span. They're found in the waters near Australia. In the Malay language, they're called *duyung*, which means "lady of the sea."

KAYAKERS

Some people think that the mermaids of Scotland and Ireland may have been traders traveling in kayaks. Just imagine what a kayaker would look like coming across the water: You'd only see the top half of their body, and the lower half would seem to be in the water. You might even imagine that it could be shaped like a fish's tail.

WHAT ARE MANATEES LIKE?

ASK *a* MANATEE BIOLOGIST!

KATIE TRIPP became fascinated with manatees when she was eleven years old, and she's spent her whole life studying them. As a marine biologist and manatee expert, she knows a few surprising facts about these gentle creatures.

How they eat: "Manatees are related to elephants. The manatee's mouth is like a very short trunk. They can do the same things with their mouth muscles"—like grabbing food—"that an elephant can do with the tip of its trunk."

How they sense their environment: "They don't have a neck they can turn. But every hair on their body is linked to a nerve. The hairs send signals to their brain."

What baby manatees look like: "In the womb, the tail is folded over the belly. They look a little bit like a bean. When they're just born, the sides of their tails are still bent."

How their breath smells: "Kind of like vegetables that are starting to rot." (Manatees are mostly vegetarian!)

Manatees' diet doesn't just give them bad breath. It also makes them fart a lot! "You'll see bubbles come to the surface—*ploop, ploop, ploop*."

ANCIENT BONES *and* "MERMAID IVORY"

GEORG WILHELM STELLER
1709–1746

MANATEES AND dugongs once had another cousin—Steller's sea cow.

In 1741, the German naturalist Georg Wilhelm Steller was shipwrecked on an Alaskan island. He was stranded there for a year, and he spent his time observing a strange animal, a type of "sea cow" that swam off the coast.

Steller's sea cows could grow to be thirty feet long. They had so much blubber, they couldn't dive underwater. They stayed close to the surface and ate a lot of kelp.

What Is Kelp?

About thirty species of brown algae are called kelp, and they all grow as seaweeds in coastal waters. The largest type of kelp can grow more than two hundred feet long!

When Steller discovered the sea cows, they were already very rare. Within thirty years, every last one had died or been killed, and they went extinct.

But the bones of Steller's sea cows can still be found on islands in Alaska. The people who live there collect them and carve them into beautiful objects. They're sometimes called mermaid ivory or mermaid bones.

MEDIEVAL MERMAIDS

BY THE eleventh century, as tales of fish-people spread, mermaids had started to become a symbol of danger for Christians. They could be found all over the place. Bestiaries—books that described all sorts of animals, real and imaginary—often included mermaids. They were shown as creatures with strange powers to attract men and make them act badly.

In this era, Christian churches used mermaids as a way to remind people to behave. In churches all over Europe—in France, Switzerland, Germany, and Italy, but especially in England and Ireland—images of mermaids were carved into pews and other wooden decorations.

These mermaids were often shown holding a mirror and a comb—symbols of the sin of vanity. They appeared to be obsessed with their own beauty. People also believed that mermaids were so charming that they were hard to resist, and could convince humans to do things they weren't supposed to. Some medieval Christians believed that mermaids wanted to capture their souls! Stories like this were a lesson. And the mermaid art reminded churchgoers not to sin.

Sometimes, in these images, a mermaid would be shown holding tight to a fish she'd captured. In Christianity, a fish is a symbol associated with Jesus Christ and Christian believers. Any religious person would get the message: Acting like a mermaid—valuing earthly beauty over spirituality—could be bad for your soul.

A church in the village of Zennor, not far from the English coast, has a bench with a famous carving of a mermaid on one end. The bench is thought to be more than five hundred years old, and there's a story that goes with it.

Centuries ago, a mysterious, beautiful woman would come to the church and sing. She had a perfect voice. Matthew Trewella was a talented singer as well. One day he followed her after church, all the way to the ocean. She revealed the truth: She was a mermaid, and if he wanted to be with her, he would have to live under the water.

The village never saw him again.

the SAD MERMAID WHO WANTED *a* SOUL

ON A small island called Iona off the coast of Scotland, a story is told about a mermaid who wanted a soul. She would swim to shore and visit the holy man who lived on the island. Every time she asked for help, he would tell her that she needed to make a trade: If she wanted a soul, she would have to leave the water, forever.

The mermaid wouldn't do that. She cried and begged, until finally she swam away and never came back. But, according to the legend, when her tears fell on land, they hardened into shiny rocks. Today on Iona, it's possible to find those special green-gray rocks, which are now called mermaid's tears.

There are two other types of mermaid's tears.

One is sea glass, created when pieces of glass fall into the ocean and are pounded smooth against the sandy shore. They look like jewels and often have a frosty, sparkling surface made of tiny crystals. Most often, they are clear, brown, and green, the colors of old bottles. It's much harder to find orange, red, and yellow sea glass. And as glass bottles have become less common than plastic, it has now become rare to find any sea glass on the beach.

These days, small pieces of plastic are sometimes called mermaid's tears, too. Plastic objects are made from nurdles—tiny particles of plastic. Millions of nurdles have made their way into the ocean. All sorts of other plastic trash that gets into the ocean breaks down into very small pieces, too. If mermaids were real, they definitely would be crying about all the plastic polluting their home.

the TALE *of the* TWO-TAILED MERMAID

AS MERMAIDS became more popular in medieval Europe, a new mermaid image appeared. This mermaid had not one tail, but two! Just below the spot where her tail started, it split in half. Usually she was shown facing forward, with her tail curling up around her, one half on each side of her body.

Two-tailed mermaids can be found on monuments in Scotland and in church carvings across Europe. It's not entirely clear why people started imagining mermaids with two tails. Sometimes the mermaids had crowns on their heads, too. Over time, these two-tailed royal mermaids were linked to a particular story about a mermaid named Melusine (say: me-loo-ZINE).

For many years, the story of Melusine was told in France, the tiny country of Luxembourg, and the neighboring region. In the late 1300s, a man named Jean d'Arras finally wrote it down, at the request of a duke. His book is titled *Melusine: or, The Noble History of Lusignan*. It is both a fairy tale and a family history, about the Lusignans of western France and their connection to a woman with magical powers.

the STORY *of* MELUSINE

THE STORY begins with a fairy named Pressina. She fell in love with a human king—a mortal!—and gave birth to triplets. She named the three girls Melior, Palatina, and Melusine. Pressina told their father he could never see his daughters while she was bathing them.

But he broke that rule, and Pressina fled with her girls. Years later, when they were fifteen years old, she told them what had happened. The sisters secretly decided to get revenge on their father. They found him and locked him up.

But when their mother found out, she was so angry that she cursed her daughters. Each one had a different punishment. Under the curse, from then on, Melusine would be forced to turn into a fish from the waist down every Saturday.

Melusine, who now spent one day a week as a mermaid, left home and started wandering the world. In the woods in France, she met a noble named Raymond and married him. Like her mother, she had one condition: He could never come into her private rooms on Saturdays. And, like her father, Raymond broke that rule and discovered she would take the form of a mermaid.

Melusine decided to forgive him. But Raymond couldn't keep what he had learned a secret. He told the whole court that his wife was a monster! Truly angry, Melusine, who had inherited a bit of magic from her fairy mother, transformed into a dragon and flew away.

MY MOTHER *the* MERMAID

THERE ARE many stories about people, like Raymond, who don't pay attention to the warnings of their local folklore and marry mermaids anyway. Sometimes they have many children. Usually, in these stories, the children eventually return to the sea with their mermaid mothers. But there are a few stories of children who stay, either because they are left behind or because a family member hides them away.

These are just stories, but there are families in Europe who say that they're descended from the marriages of humans and mermaids. Certain Irish families—the O'Byrnes, the O'Cullens, and the MacInerneys, for instance—have mermaids in their family crests.

Other families have names that hint they're descended from sea people. The MacNamaras of County Clare are supposed to have mermaids in their family, and *MacNamara* means "son of the sea."

People with mermaid ancestors are thought to have special powers. They might have webbed fingers, like a frog. And they may be "charmers"—using their supernatural skills, they could stop blood from flowing or cure certain sicknesses.

Even royal families wanted to be connected to mermaids. Some royal families in Europe claim they're descended from Melusine! The House of Lusignan in France and the House of Luxembourg both include Melusine among their ancestors.

CITY *of* MERMAIDS

IN THE Middle Ages, a mermaid became the official symbol of the city of Warsaw, Poland.

A mermaid-like creature first appeared on the city's coat of arms all the way back in 1390. Like the original sirens, it had wings and bird legs. But more than two hundred years later, the image of this creature had transformed into a mermaid, with a human body and fish tail. She held a shield and a sword to help her protect the city.

Why did Warsaw choose a mermaid? There's a legend that a mermaid once washed up on the banks of the Wisła River, which runs through the city. The fishermen there fell in love with her. When a merchant captured her and held her prisoner, the fishermen rescued her. To thank them, she swore to protect their city.

The people of Warsaw call their mermaid Syrenka (just like the sirens). There are statues and carvings of her all over Warsaw, including a towering statue that was placed in the town square in 1855.

SEARCHING *for the* TRUTH ABOUT MERMAIDS

BY THE eighteenth century, scientists and government officials wanted to know: Did mermaids really exist?

In 1723, a royal commission from Denmark started to look for real evidence. If they couldn't find any, their government would start punishing anyone who mentioned mermaids.

The commission sailed to the Faroe Islands, a remote land where mermaids had been spotted. The islands sit in the North Atlantic Ocean. There, they reported that they saw a merman looking straight at them! They also heard a story from ferrymen closer to Denmark who said they had seen a merman. According to these men, the merman blew out a puff of air and roared before he disappeared.

Denmark's government was convinced that merpeople could be real, but others kept looking.

Carl Linnaeus, a Swedish scientist, spent his whole life trying to identify and name plants and animals. He was fascinated with mermaids and hoped someone would catch one so he could study it.

The closest he ever came was a large amphibian sent to him in Europe from North Carolina. The people in North Carolina called it a "mud iguana." Although it looked a lot like an eel, it had two small forearms, like a lizard. Inside, Linnaeus found that it had gills, like a fish, and lungs, like a human! It reminded him enough of a mermaid that he gave it the scientific name *Siren lacertina*.

There are only two other living members of the *Siren* genus of animals. One, *Siren reticulata*, can grow up to two feet long. It's also called a leopard eel, and it was first identified by scientists in 2018. The *Siren intermedia*—known as a mud eel or a lesser siren—is much more common.

the PRIEST WHO DRESSED UP *as a* MERMAID

ROBERT S. HAWKER was a poet, a priest, and an unusual man, with a unique way of dressing. He hated wearing black and often wore a purple coat, a blue sweater, and fishing boots. He cared deeply for the people of his village in Cornwall, England. But he also loved practical jokes.

According to local lore, one summer night sometime in the 1820s, Hawker rowed out to a rock near the seashore. He brought with him a sheet of dark waterproof canvas and a mirror. While sitting on the rock, he wrapped the sheet around his legs so that it looked like a tail. He used seaweed to make a wig. Then he started singing loudly and waving the mirror around.

Soon, people heard the noise and came to the beach. In the moonlit night, they saw a mermaid sitting on the rock! Eventually, Hawker disappeared into the water and secretly made his way back to the village. But he returned to the rock the next night and the next.

The crowds kept growing, but after several nights, the joke started getting old. On the last night, Hawker sang "God Save the King," the national anthem of Britain, then swam away. Many people in the village were sure they had seen a real mermaid.

Hawker's son-in-law recorded this story in a book about the priest's life and said he confirmed it with witnesses from the village. But, like mermaids themselves, this story may be more legend than fact. Robert S. Hawker was an unconventional man. But we may never know for sure if he really posed as a mermaid.

a MERMAID *in* LONDON

DURING THE nineteenth century fake mermaids seemed to be everywhere.

In 1822, Captain Samuel Barrett Eades bought a stuffed mermaid in the city of Batavia (today called Jakarta, in Indonesia). Dried and wrinkled, it had black skin, thin hair, clawlike fingers, and a horrible look on its face. It cost so much, he had to sell an entire ship to afford it.

That autumn, back in London, Captain Eades rented his own small space inside a coffee shop. He kept the mermaid under a glass dome and charged one shilling to see it. For months, the mermaid had many visitors, including famous writers and scientists. *Finally*, they thought, *proof that mermaids exist!*

But a few people weren't so sure. Experts who examined the mermaid figured out that it was a fake. It had been made with parts of a fish and a monkey, joined together so well that it was almost impossible to tell.

Soon, all of London was laughing at the fake mermaid, and no one was paying to see it anymore. But Captain Eades needed money. He had been betting on the success of the mermaid; the ship he had sold to buy it wasn't even his! When he couldn't pay the owner back, he had to work for them without pay for the rest of his life.

the FAKE MERMAID *in* NEW YORK

TWENTY YEARS later, in 1842, Captain Eades's mermaid became famous once again. This time, it had a new name: the Feejee Mermaid.

The Republic of Fiji—spelled *Feejee* in the nineteenth century—is a group of islands in the South Pacific. The mermaid didn't come from there, but Europeans and Americans weren't always careful about the details of geography in foreign places. To them, *Feejee* just meant "somewhere far away." In reality, Fiji and Jakarta, where Captain Eades actually bought the mermaid, are almost five thousand miles away from each other!

When Captain Eades died, his son sold the fake mermaid to a Boston museum owner, who showed it to P. T. Barnum, the great showman and circus master. Barnum knew just what to do with it.

One day shortly after, a man who called himself Dr. J. Griffin showed up at an inn in Philadelphia. He just happened to show the owner what he had brought with him—a small stuffed mermaid. Soon, word got around, and everyone in Philadephia seemed to have heard about it. But Dr. Griffin kept the mermaid locked up and wouldn't show it to the public.

Instead, he traveled to New York City. The story was mysteriously being told there as well. People wanted to know if the mermaid really existed. All the New York newspapers wanted to see the mermaid, too. Finally, Dr. Griffin agreed to show a few reporters. After every newspaper in the city had written something sensational about the mermaid, the announcement came out—P. T. Barnum would be allowed to display it.

This had been the plan the whole time. "Dr. Griffin"—a fake name—actually worked for Barnum! By keeping the Feejee Mermaid hidden, they had made everyone so curious about it that crowds of people couldn't wait to see it. For months, Barnum made money showing the mermaid in New York and, later, all around the country. In the US, no one seemed to care if Captain Eades's London mermaid was fake or not.

the ART *of the* FAKE

THE FEEJEE Mermaid wasn't unique. It originally came from Japan, where artists produced many creatures like it. Inspired by the myth of the *ningyo*, the fake mermaids were made of fish parts, animals, papier-mâché, wood, and wire. They always had frightening faces.

And Captain Eades wasn't the first person to display a fake mermaid in Europe. For years, there was a "mermaid's skeleton" on display in Copenhagen, Denmark. Another London man claimed to own a mermaid's hand, and eighteenth century fairs sometimes showed "mermaids" as one of their attractions.

There's another type of fake mermaid, too, called a Jenny Haniver. (No one knows exactly where the name came from.) These are made from skates and rays, which have flat bodies and flat fins attached to their sides like wings. On their undersides, skates have two nostrils and a mouth.

Jenny Hanivers are made from dead, dried skates, with nostrils and mouth shaped to look more like a human face. Other parts of the fish's body are also posed to look more like a mermaid. In the end, though, they usually look more like a small dragon or an alien!

Skates and Rays

- Skates and rays are both types of fish and are related to sharks.
- Rays give birth to live baby rays.
- Skates produce their young inside an egg case, known as a mermaid's purse.

WHAT'S INSIDE *a* MERMAID'S PURSE?

WALKING ALONG a beach, you might find a "mermaid's purse." It will look like a small pod or wallet—a dark rectangular packet with a thick thread attached to each corner. Mermaid's purses are cases for skate eggs and for some shark eggs! (Of the eight orders of sharks, only three—bullhead sharks, carpet sharks, and ground sharks—have species who create egg cases.)

These cases are made of collagen, a protein found in your skin, too. Most have just one egg inside. Each shark or skate makes an egg case of a different size and shape. Some have thick "horns" on each corner, and others have thinner curly threads. The threads attach to seaweed or the ocean floor, keeping the egg cases from floating free through the ocean.

Some of the eggs spend a whole year inside the egg case. The baby sharks first hatch inside the case and can be seen swimming inside, until one end opens up, and the tiny baby swims free. The empty cases wash up on shore. Occasionally, a storm causes a strong enough current to rip them from the seafloor and send them to the beach with an egg or baby shark still inside.

HANS CHRISTIAN ANDERSEN

OF ALL the stories ever told about mermaids, the most famous one was written by Hans Christian Andersen. He lived in Denmark, a country surrounded by water on three sides. He was born to a poor family. But as a young man, he found people who believed in him and helped pay for his education.

While he was still in college, Andersen became a very popular writer. Most of his books took events from his own life and turned them into stories. But in 1835, he started publishing fairy tales—some of the most well-known in history.

Some of Andersen's stories, like "The Princess and the Pea," were based on folktales that he grew up with. Others, like "The Emperor's New Clothes," were retellings of stories from other parts of the world. But some—like "The Ugly Duckling" and "The Little Match Girl"—were all his own.

He wrote more than 165 fairy tales in all, and many have become famous throughout the world.

Andersen published "The Little Mermaid" in 1837, and it was one of his first tales to appear in English, in 1846. It's still among his most popular stories, and part of the reason he's known as the most important fairy-tale writer of his time.

the LITTLE MERMAID

IN HANS CHRISTIAN ANDERSEN'S original telling, the story of the Little Mermaid begins "far out in the ocean" in the realm of a sea king. Each of the king's six daughters gets the chance to visit the surface when she turns fifteen. When the youngest has her turn, she falls in love with a prince, rescues him from a shipwreck, and leaves him on dry land. There, a young woman who lives in a sacred temple near the ocean finds him and brings him home.

The mermaid can't stop thinking about the prince, and she drinks a potion made by a sea witch so she can be with the prince on land. The potion turns her tail into human legs. But there's a cost. She can never return to being a mermaid. She can no longer speak or sing. And her new feet are very painful.

When she finally meets the prince, they spend every day together. Once, he even kisses her. But he tells the mermaid that he can only marry the young woman who found him at the temple—the girl he believes rescued him from the sea.

The mermaid knows she's actually the one who saved the prince, but she has no way to tell him. She travels with him to a nearby kingdom, where his parents have arranged his marriage. He promises the mermaid he won't go through with it—until they arrive, and he finds that the person he's supposed to marry is the same young woman who found him at the temple.

The mermaid's heart breaks. She throws herself into the sea, and her body dissolves into sea foam. But her spirit rises up into the air, where she learns she has the chance to earn a soul by doing good deeds and protecting people on Earth.

a MERMAID *in* COPENHAGEN

ONE EVENING in 1909, a brewer named Carl Jacobsen went to see a ballet of "The Little Mermaid" performed in Copenhagen, the capital of Denmark. He thought the story and the dancing were beautiful, and he wanted to celebrate them.

Jacobsen hired a sculptor, Edvard Eriksen, to create a statue of the Little Mermaid. Made of bronze and granite, the statue has two legs that end in fins. She sits on a rock with a thoughtful look on her face. (It's modeled after the face of the dancer who performed the mermaid's part in the ballet.) The piece, just four feet tall, was placed by the waterside in 1913.

At first, the mermaid statue was mostly ignored. But in the 1930s, Danish leaders wanted to change how outsiders thought of their country. They started pointing out that it was a peaceful place—a fairy-tale land, of sorts. The Little Mermaid was a perfect symbol of this new idea.

Today, the mermaid has become one of the most visited places in the city of Copenhagen. And it's so well-known that it's been copied many times. Other mermaid statues can be found in California, Spain, South Korea, Canada, and other places around the world.

the FIRST MOVIE MERMAID

JUST AS the Copenhagen statue was becoming famous, so was a movie mermaid.

Annette Kellermann was born in Australia in 1886 and began swimming as a young girl. While still in high school, Annette performed at an amusement park, swimming in a tank with fish, sometimes twice a day. In her twenties, she took her mermaid show on a tour around the United States. Soon, she was appearing in movies, too. One of her early roles, in 1911, was in a film called *The Mermaid.*

At that time, most women went swimming in awkward "bathing costumes" that weren't so different from regular clothes. But Annette started wearing a one-piece bathing suit that was much easier to swim in—and much tighter. At first, her outfit upset some people. She was even arrested in Massachusetts for wearing it! But soon she had her own line of swimsuits, and they became popular everywhere.

In her films, Annette wore mermaid tails that she designed herself. No other actress had ever before been filmed swimming in a mermaid costume. She would act out scenes underwater and do tricks that no one else could. She even dove off waterfalls! She was one of the first movie stars to become famous for her athletic ability. Everyone called her "The Australian Mermaid."

the DIFFICULT JOB *of* BEING *a* MERMAID

IN 1947, Newton Perry, who trained some of the Navy's best swimmers, built a theater at Weeki Wachee Springs, Florida, the deepest freshwater cave system in the United States. He hired young women to swim underwater and perform tricks. At every show, they would have a "mermaid picnic," eating a banana and sipping a soda underwater! For decades, these performing mermaids have put on shows at Weeki Wachee every day.

Today, the mermaid shows last for thirty minutes. Usually when people stay underwater for that long, they carry air tanks to help them breathe. But the giant Weeki Wachee tanks have special hoses that the mermaids can sip air from, as if they were drinking from a giant straw.

It's not easy to be cast as a mermaid. To pass the first audition, you need to swim three hundred yards as quickly as you can and tread water for ten minutes.

New mermaids at Weeki Wachee have to train for six months to a year, and then work four days a week. Sometimes they travel and perform in tanks elsewhere, too. Most mermaids eventually give up swimming for life back on land, but one, Vicki Smith, started in 1957 and sixty years later still sometimes performed with other former mermaids.

HOW CAN MERMAIDS BREATHE UNDERWATER?

ASK *a* BIOLOGIST!

THIS IS one of the great mysteries about mermaids. If they are supposed to be part fish and part human, do they have gills . . . or lungs . . . or both?

According to Michael Berenbrink, a biologist who studies animal respiratory systems, there's a core difference between water breathers and air breathers. Both types of animals need oxygen. But air has much more oxygen than water—thirty times more! So animals that breathe water need to do a much better job of passing it through their breathing organs.

"It's very hard work, really," says Berenbrink. "It's not really efficient to do it like mammals do it, to breathe in and breathe out." It's much less work to let water continuously flow over gills. So a mermaid would definitely need gills.

The human half of the mermaid would probably react to being deep underwater the same way a deep-diving seal or whale does. Her heart would beat slowly, and the blood would concentrate around her most important organs—her hearts, lungs, and brain, which need oxygen the most.

What would happen when a mermaid came on land? If she ever wanted to use her gills again, she would need to keep them moist. (Dried-out gills stick together and can't be separated, making them useless.) She would also need lungs—or something like them—to breathe.

There are animals, such as the lungfish, that spend time in the water and on land, and have the ability to breathe in both water and air. The strange thing, though, is that mermaids are never pictured with gills. Where could they be hiding them?

Lungfish

FREE DIVING

LIKE OCEAN-DWELLING mammals, some people can swim deep underwater on just one breath of air.

This is called free diving, and it takes special training. It might be the closest a human can come to experiencing the ocean as a mermaid would. In free diving competitions, divers plunge hundreds of feet deep on a single breath.

At the beginning of the dive, a free diver has to work to swim deeper and deeper. But at around sixty feet underwater, they will start free-falling under the pressure of the water above. Some use weights to pull them down. Others go only as far as they can using just the weight of their own body.

Free diving can be very dangerous. A swimmer needs to keep their mind very quiet and to control their breathing. Even trained free divers can only stay underwater for a short amount of time, but while they're there, they can explore the sea without any special equipment.

There are free divers who don't care about diving as deep as they can or breaking records. Some free divers go underwater to explore sunken ships or take pictures. In Japan and Korea, there is a long tradition of free diving for food—lobsters, sea urchins, abalone—or for pearls!

MERMAID TAILS

BESIDES THE Weeki Wachee mermaids, there are hundreds of working professional mermaids. They perform at birthday parties, weddings, and aquariums. They work as underwater models. Some have their own video channels online. And their most important possessions are their tails.

At their simplest, mermaid tails are made of fabric, just like swimsuits. They are printed with patterns that look like fish scales. Some have flippers inside.

A professional mermaid needs a much fancier tail. These tails are made of a type of flexible plastic called silicone, and they're sculpted to the mermaid's body. They look like they're real, and they cost thousands of dollars!

Being a mermaid is a special skill. Wearing a mermaid tail means that it's much more difficult to use your legs while swimming. Professional mermaids train hundreds of hours in order to be able to swim safely with their tails. So while it's easy to buy a mermaid tail, it's much harder to become a true mermaid, who can swim easily while wearing one.

the CONEY ISLAND MERMAID PARADE

ONCE A year, in New York City, anyone can be a mermaid. Each June, thousands of people dress up like mermaids, mermen, and many other sea creatures and march in the Coney Island Mermaid Parade.

Coney Island is right on the Atlantic Ocean, in the borough of Brooklyn, and one of its main streets is named Mermaid Avenue. Another is Neptune Avenue, named after a mythical god of the sea. On the boardwalk, there are roller coasters, carnival games, musicians, magicians, and much more to see.

In 1983, a local organization started the Mermaid Parade to celebrate artistic New Yorkers. Every year, mermaids walk the parade route wearing tails, crowns, glitter, and seashells, with brightly colored hair and body paint. Among them, a King Neptune and Queen Mermaid, chosen each year, ride down the street in style. Hundreds of thousands of people crowd onto the sidewalks to watch the parade.

The whole event ends on the beach, where there's a ceremony to welcome the summer. And whoever has the best costume wins a prize!

MODERN MOVIE MERMAIDS

IN THE 1980s, moviemakers created two of the most memorable mermaids in modern history.

In *Splash*, which came out in 1984, a mermaid named Madison and a man named Allen fall in love. The only problem: He doesn't know she's a mermaid! She rescues him from drowning twice, once when he's a boy and again, twenty years later. The second time she rescues him, she decides to come on land and try to find him again. When Madison's legs are dry, they look like human legs. But if her legs get wet, she turns back into a mermaid.

She's also in danger. A scientist knows she's a mermaid and is trying to prove it. When he splashes water on her legs, her secret is revealed, and she is snatched away by the government. Allen races to rescue her, and in the end they dive into the ocean. Madison gives Allen the power to breathe underwater, and they swim away to live together the rest of their lives.

The most well-known movie mermaid of all is Ariel, from Disney's *The Little Mermaid.* She has bright red hair and is obsessed with human culture and collecting objects from shipwrecks. The movie is based on Hans Christian Andersen's story, but there are some important differences.

Just as in the story, Ariel rescues a handsome prince named Eric and falls in love with him. But in the movie, before she returns to the ocean, she sings to him and leaves him with a memory of her beautiful voice.

In order to join the prince on land, Ariel makes a deal with Ursula the sea witch. She trades her voice for a pair of legs. (Unlike in Andersen's story, her new legs don't hurt her.) She has just three days to make the prince fall in love with her.

And it works. Even without hearing her voice, the prince almost kisses her. But the sea witch never meant for Ariel to succeed, and she's angry that the little mermaid is doing so well. Ursula turns herself human and, using Ariel's voice, tries to steal the prince.

In this version of the story, the little mermaid wins. Eric helps defeat the sea witch, and Ariel's father, King Triton, finally accepts that his daughter will be happier living as a human. He turns her tail back into legs, and Ariel chooses to stay on land and marry the prince.

SIGN *of the* MERMAID

IN THE 1600s, there was a well-known bar called the Mermaid Tavern in London. Some of the wisest and wittiest men in the city would meet there every month to laugh, argue, and trade secrets.

Shakespeare and His Friends at the Mermaid Tavern

Over the years, many other Mermaid Taverns and Mermaid Inns have featured signs proudly displaying a mermaid. One of the most famous mermaid signs in the world is the Starbucks logo.

In the early 1970s, the first Starbucks coffee shop opened in Seattle, Washington. Seattle is a port city, and the shop was named after a character—the first mate—in the great American novel *Moby-Dick*. The owners wanted a logo that would make their customers think of the sea. Inspired by an old image of a two-tailed mermaid, they put a mermaid wearing a crown in the center of their sign.

Over time, the Starbucks mermaid has changed her look. The logo went from brown to green. But you can still see the ends of her two tails, one on either side of her head.

MERMAID FOODS

IN 2017, a café in New York City that had become famous for creating a Unicorn Latte invented a new drink—the Merbabe Latte.

This drink was bright pink, with light blue foam on top. It was covered in sparkling sprinkles and had a pink mermaid's tail sticking out of it. This latte was made with dragon fruit and special bright red berries. It also had blue-green algae and bits of kelp in it!

That year, Starbucks also made a mermaid drink—a Mermaid Frappuccino. Made of milk, vanilla, and blackberries, it was also pink, with a sprinkle of green matcha—powdered green tea.

Here are a few other mermaid foods that might be spotted on land:

MERMAID TOAST: Found mostly online. Cream cheese, dyed blue and green with food coloring or edible algae, is spread on toasted bread to look like ocean waves.

MERMAID SMOOTHIE BOWLS: Restricted habitat. Generally blue, due to edible algae powder, swirled into a banana–coconut milk smoothie. Topped with fruit and nuts, and found most often in expensive cafés.

MERMAID CAKE: Common. Any sea-themed cake can be a mermaid cake. There are many ways to make a mermaid cake, but one easy idea is to add candy seashells and a premade mermaid tail!

MARSHMALLOW MERMAID PIE: Rare. In the movie *Waitress*, the main character makes a mermaid pie with marshmallow filling, whipped cream, and rainbow-colored mini marshmallows on top.

MERMAID PYE: Endangered. This is a very different type of pie! All the way back in the seventeenth century, cooks made "mermaid pye" by baking a small piglet in a crust. Sometimes it had cow's tongue or eel in it, too, along with butter, bacon, and spices.

WHO EATS SEAWEED?

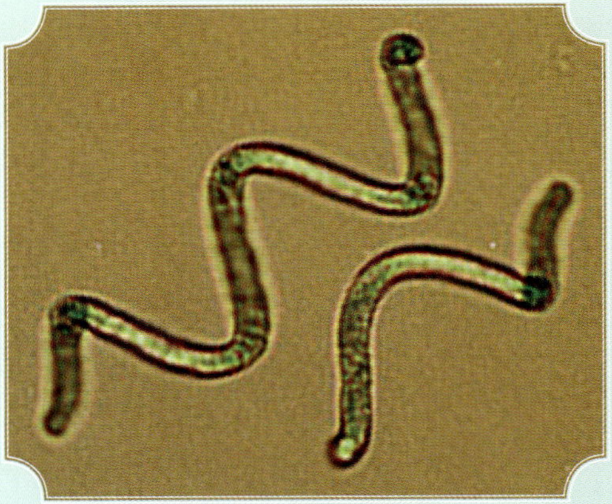

MANY MERMAID foods made today are colored blue-green using a bacteria called spirulina. These tiny organisms grow all over the world, in lakes, ponds, seawater, springs, and marshes. A big group of them looks like a mat spreading over the top of the water. But under a microscope, they look like tiny perfect spirals.

People have been using spirulina as food for centuries. In the 1400s, Europeans who traveled to Mexico found that people there would harvest spirulina from a large lake, dry it into greenish cakes, and eat it. Across the Atlantic Ocean, in Chad, a country in Africa, people still made spirulina cakes in the same way in the twentieth century.

In addition to turning smoothies a very pretty color, spirulina has many vitamins. It tastes a little bit earthy, which not everyone likes!

Technically, spirulina isn't a plant, but it is a living organism. There are many types of edible water plants, however, that people eat. From Japan and Korea to Iceland and Ireland, seaweed has been an important food for hundreds of years.

Today, one of the most common uses of seaweed worldwide is in Japanese food—the dark sheets of nori that are used to wrap rolls of sushi are made from seaweed pressed into sheets and dried. Kombu is dried kelp that's used in Japanese soups. Another type of seaweed, wakame, is often added to miso soup.

In Ireland, people collect a type of seaweed called dulse, a red algae, from along the coastline, dry it, and eat it. Some people like to fry it first. It's supposed to taste like bacon!

MERMAID HAIR

IN MYTHS, mermaids' hair might be black, silvery, blond, brown, or seaweed green. And Ariel's hair in *The Little Mermaid* is bright red.

Now, mermaid hair usually means long, wavy hair dyed a combination of blue, green, and purple.

In 2015, mermaid hair got a giant boost when Disney fans shared the pictures of their dyed hair on social media, in honor of the twenty-sixth anniversary of *The Little Mermaid* movie. There are no hard-and-fast rules about mermaid hair—the pictures that *Little Mermaid* fans posted were sea-algae green, deep blue, or even pastel pink. Mermaid hair can be short or long, curly or straight. The hair dyes that create these colors have names like Atomic Turquoise, Sea Nymph, and Neon Blue.

One of the first hair artists to create mermaid hair used a special technique. She would spread out the hair of the mermaid-to-be on a flat surface and paint it, by hand, with many colors of hair dye. This process could take a very long time! But there's an easier way to get mermaid hair, which anyone can try.

DIY MERMAID HAIR

TO EXPERIMENT with glorious mermaid hair, try using hair chalk. (It'll wash out with water and shampoo.)

You'll need:

- A pack of hair chalk
- An old T-shirt
- A paper plate (to rest the chalk on)
- A spray bottle filled with water
- A hair dryer
- Dishwashing gloves
- A grown-up helper

To get mermaid hair:

1. Put on the old T-shirt. (The chalk can stain clothes.)
2. Divide your hair into sections. You want to color the top sections, so that people can see it! (And also, if you keep the chalk off the bottom layers, it will help keep your clothes clean.)
3. Wet your hair with water from the spray bottle. Or ask your helper to spray your hair for you.
4. Put on your gloves.
5. If your hair is darker, first cover the sections you want to color with white or light chalk. Use a downward motion.
6. Ask your helper to color a third of the sections green, a third blue, and a third purple.
7. Dry your hair to help the chalk set.
8. Remember to take a picture!

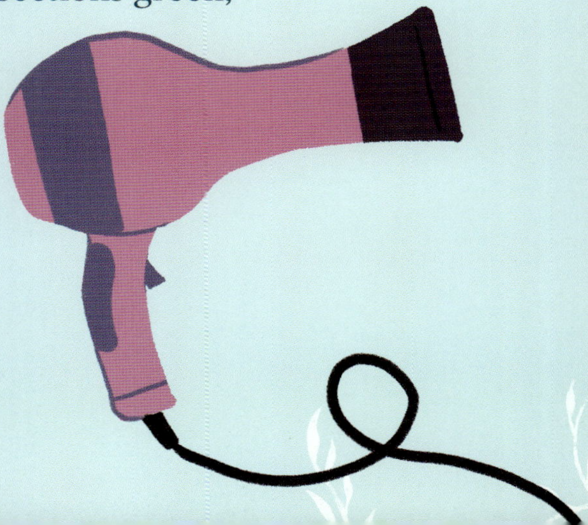

the OTHER KIND *of* MERMAID'S HAIR

IN THE ocean, mermaid's hair has a different meaning—it's a type of algae! There are a few types of seaweed with long strands that look a lot like hair. They're known by names like mermaid's hair, mermaid's tresses, or mermaid's fan.

Mermaid's hair: More than one type of algae is called mermaid's hair—brown algae with light, feathery tendrils; thicker, clumpier green algae; or a deep-red algae.

Mermaid's tresses: This is a brown algae with thicker strands that look like spaghetti!

Mermaid's fan: This algae grows into the shape of a leaf or a fan—it's bright green and looks like the perfect accessory for mermaids.

MERMAID CROWNS

IN DISNEY'S *The Little Mermaid*, King Triton has a five-pointed golden crown. Some of Ariel's older sisters wear crowns, too. The Starbucks mermaid wears a crown. Sometimes Melusine is shown with one, as well. Mermaids don't always wear crowns, but what makes a perfect crown for a mermaid?

Today, artists who make and sell mermaid crowns often craft them from dozens of small shells. Chelsea Shiels, a designer in Australia, started making crowns like these because she liked the way they looked. Her mermaid crowns are beautiful creations of sparkling jewels and pointed shells. (But when other people saw them, they loved them, and soon she was making as many as she could.)

For each crown, she uses anywhere from twenty to fifty shells, and she is very careful about where she buys them.

Shell Alert!

Seashells once were the homes of living creatures, and in some parts of the world, people kill those animals just to get their shells. That can harm beach environments and make life harder for the creatures that still live there. Every year, thousands upon thousands of shells are sold as souvenirs and jewelry, and it's important when buying a shell to know where it came from.

Even collecting shells off a beach can be bad for other living things. Some animals leave their empty shell behind so that smaller animals can move in.

Mermaid crowns don't have to have shells on them! They can be made of shining crystals, pearls, coral branches, tiny starfish, beads, gems, and glitter, or colorful gleaming metal, like the crowns in *The Little Mermaid*.

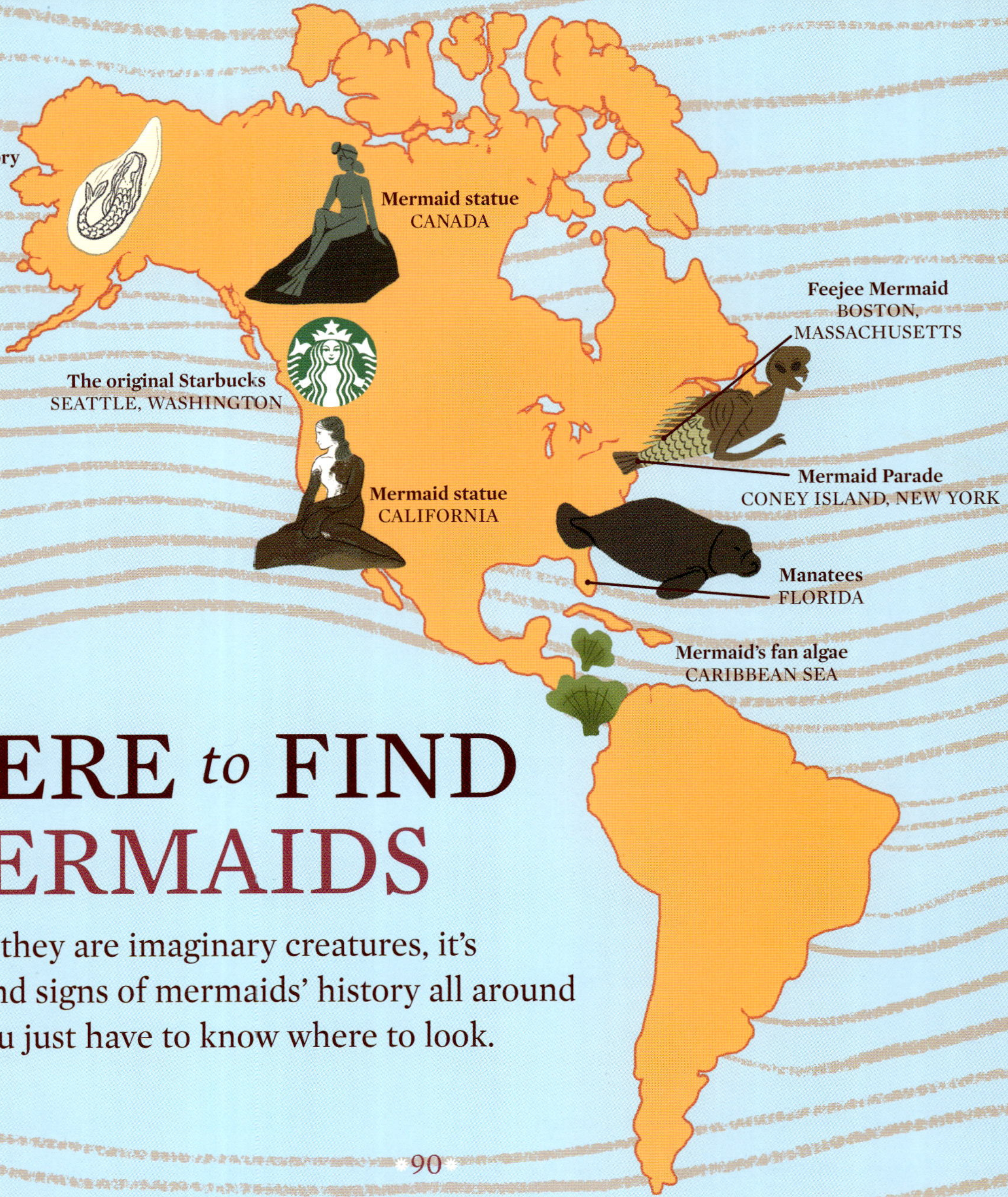

WHERE *to* FIND MERMAIDS

Even though they are imaginary creatures, it's possible to find signs of mermaids' history all around the world. You just have to know where to look.

Mermaid's tears
IONA, SCOTLAND
Mermaid statue
COPENHAGEN, DENMARK
Syrenka
WARSAW, POLAND
Church carvings
IRELAND & ENGLAND
Mermaid statue
SPAIN
African manatees
SENEGAL
Mermaid statue
SOUTH KOREA
Mermaid bones
JAPAN
Dugongs
MALAYSIA

BIBLIOGRAPHY

*Books for young readers

*Andersen, Hans Christian. "The Little Mermaid." ***The Complete Andersen.*** New York: Heritage Press, 1949.

Benwell, Gwen, and Arthur Waugh. ***Sea Enchantress: The Tale of the Mermaid and Her Kin.*** New York: Citadel Press, 1965.

Bondeson, Jan. ***The Feejee Mermaid and Other Essays in Natural and Unnatural History.*** Ithaca: Cornell University Press, 1999.

Higgins, Jim. ***Irish Mermaids: Sirens, Temptresses and their Symbolism in Art, Architecture and Folklore.*** Galway: Crow's Rock Press, 1995.

Pedersen, Tara E. ***Mermaids and the Production of Knowledge in Early Modern England.*** New York: Routledge, 2016.

Philpotts, Beatrice. ***Mermaids.*** New York: Ballantine Books, 1980.

*Skerry, Brian. ***Face to Face with Manatees.*** Washington, DC: National Geographic Society, 2010.

Turgeon, Carolyn. ***The Mermaid Handbook.*** New York: Harper Design, 2018.